The Diabetic Cake Cookbook

© Copyright 2023. Laura Sommers.
All rights reserved.
No part of this book may be reproduced in any form or by any electronic or mechanical means without written permission of the author. All text, illustrations and design are the exclusive property of
Laura Sommers

Introduction	1
Chocolate Layer Cake	2
Blackberry Shortcake	4
Chocolate Eclaire Cake	6
Strawberry Shortcake	7
Whipped Topping	8
Caramel Cupcakes	9
Coffee Crumb Cake	10
Boston Cream Napoleon	12
Tiramisu	13
Pineapple Upside Down Cake	14
Vanilla Coconut Cake	15
Chocolate Pudding Cake	16
Gingerbread Cupcakes	17
Pumpkin Spice Cake	18
Almond Cake	19
Berry Sponge Cake	20
Angel Food Cake	21
Peach Cake	22
Little Italy Cake	23
Carrot Cake	24
Red Velvet Cake	25
Vanilla Pound Cake	26

Key Lime Cake 27

Yellow Cake 29

Hummingbird Cake: 30

Diabetic Lemon Cake 32

Diabetic Banana Cake 33

Diabetic Vanilla Cake 34

Blueberry Coffee Cake 35

Apple Cinnamon Diabetic Cake 36

Lemon Poppy Seed Cake 37

Almond Flour Coffee Cake 38

Peanut Butter Chocolate Chip Cake 39

Raspberry Coconut Cake 40

Chocolate Zucchini Cake 41

Chocolate Almond Cake 42

Cherry Almond Cake 43

Apricot Almond Cake 44

Black Forest Cake 45

Chocolate Cherry Cake 47

Pistachio Cake 48

Cookies 'n' Cream Cupcakes 49

Orange Dream Angel Cake 51

Diabetic Chocolate Cherry Cola Poke Cake 52

Diabetic Oatmeal Coffee Cake 53

Diabetic Mocha Cake 54

Diabetic Strawberry Cream Cake 55

Diabetic Cranberry Orange Cake 56

Lemon Ricotta Cake 57

Chocolate Chip Cheesecake Cupcakes 58

Peanut Butter Lava Cupcakes 59

Diabetic Apple Spice Cake 60

Lemon Yogurt Cake 61

Diabetic Vanilla Orange Cake 62

Diabetic Chocolate Mint Cake 63

Diabetic Chocolate Hazelnut Cake 64

Diabetic Lemon Lavender Cake 65

Diabetic Caramel Apple Cake 66

Chocolate Cherry Cola Poke Cake 67

Diabetic Toffee Chocolate Cake 68

About the Author 69

Other Books by Laura Sommers 70

Introduction

Welcome to our cookbook for diabetic cakes! Living with diabetes can be challenging, especially when it comes to indulging in sweet treats. However, with the right ingredients and techniques, it's possible to enjoy delicious cakes without compromising your health.

In this cookbook, we've gathered a collection of recipes that are specifically designed for people with diabetes.

Our aim is to show that you can still enjoy the pleasure of baked goods while keeping your blood sugar levels under control. Each recipe is carefully crafted to minimize the use of sugar and carbohydrates, and to maximize the use of low-glycemic index ingredients that won't cause spikes in blood sugar.

Whether you're a diabetic or simply looking for healthier dessert options, we hope that this cookbook will inspire you to try out new recipes and discover the joy of guilt-free baking.

Chocolate Layer Cake

Cake Ingredients:

2 1/4 cups almond flour
3/4 cup cocoa powder
1/2 cup granulated erythritol (I used Swerve)
1/2 cup vanilla whey protein powder
1 tbsp instant coffee
2 tsp baking powder
1 tsp baking soda
1 tsp xanthan gum
1/2 tsp salt
6 oz Greek yogurt, room temperature
1/2 cup butter, softened
5 large eggs, room temperature
1/4 tsp stevia extract
2/3 cup almond milk

Sour Cream Frosting Ingredients:

4 oz unsweetened chocolate, chopped
1 1/2 cups sour cream, room temperature
3 cups powdered erythritol (I used Swerve)
1/4 cup cocoa powder
1 tsp vanilla extract
1/8 tsp stevia extract
1 1/2 tsp xanthan gum

Cake Directions:

1. Preheat the oven to 325 degrees F and grease 2 8-inch round cake pans.
2. Line cake pans with parchment paper and grease the parchment.
3. In a large bowl, whisk together almond flour, cocoa powder, protein powder, granulated erythritol, instant coffee, baking powder, baking soda, xanthan gum and salt.
4. In another large bowl, beat Greek yogurt and butter together until combined.
5. Beat in eggs and stevia extract.

6. Beat in almond flour mixture in two additions, alternating with almond milk, and scraping down beaters and sides of bowl as needed.
7. Divide batter between prepared pans and bake 30 to 35 minutes or until cakes are set and a tester inserted in center comes out clean.
8. Let cool in pans 10 minutes, and then flip out onto wire racks to cool completely.
9. Once cool, use a large serrated knife to cut each layer in half horizontally to create 4 layers total.

Frosting Directions:

1. In a small saucepan over low heat, melt chocolate and stir until smooth.
2. Set aside.
3. In large bowl, beat sour cream and powdered erythritol until smooth.
4. Beat in cocoa powder, then vanilla extract and stevia extract.
5. Sprinkle xanthan gum over mixture and beat in until frosting thickens slightly.
6. Stir in melted chocolate, scraping down sides of bowl, until well combined.
7. Place one layer of cake on serving platter and top with 1/2 to 3/4 cup frosting, using knife or offset spatula to spread evenly.
8. Repeat with remaining layers and frosting. For final layer, top with any remaining frosting and spread down and over sides of cake, smoothing with knife or offset spatula. If desired, use back of small spoon to create swirled effect on top of cake.
9. Chill cake in refrigerator for at least one hour. Any leftover cake should be wrapped in plastic and kept in refrigerator.
10. Place one layer of cake on serving platter and top with 1/2 to 3/4 cup frosting, using knife or offset spatula to spread evenly.
11. Repeat with remaining layers and frosting. For final layer, top with any remaining frosting and spread down and over sides of cake, smoothing with knife or offset spatula. If desired, use back of small spoon to create swirled effect on top of cake.
12. Chill cake in refrigerator for at least one hour. Any leftover cake should be wrapped in plastic and kept in refrigerator.

Blackberry Shortcake

Ingredients:
1 cup all-purpose flour
1/2 cup whole wheat flour
2 tsps. baking powder
1/2 tsp. salt
1/4 cup unsalted butter, chilled and cut into small pieces
1/4 cup unsweetened applesauce
1/4 cup low-fat milk
2 tbsps. honey
1 tsp. vanilla extract
2 cups fresh blackberries
2 tbsps. lemon juice
1 tbsp. cornstarch
1/4 cup sugar-free whipped topping

Directions:
1. Preheat the oven to 400 degrees F.
2. Line a baking sheet with parchment paper.
3. In a large bowl, whisk together the all-purpose flour, whole wheat flour, baking powder, and salt.
4. Using a pastry blender or two knives, cut in the butter until the mixture resembles coarse crumbs.
5. In a separate bowl, whisk together the applesauce, milk, honey, and vanilla extract.
6. Pour the wet ingredients into the dry ingredients and stir until just combined.
7. Turn the dough out onto a lightly floured surface and knead gently for a few seconds.
8. Roll the dough out into a 1/2-inch-thick circle and cut into 6 wedges.
9. Place the wedges on the prepared baking sheet and bake for 15-20 minutes or until golden brown.
10. While the shortcakes are baking, prepare the blackberry topping.
11. In a medium saucepan, combine the blackberries, lemon juice, and cornstarch.
12. Cook over medium heat for 5-7 minutes or until the mixture has thickened.

13. Remove from heat and let cool slightly.
14. To assemble, place a shortcake on a plate and top with a spoonful of the blackberry mixture and a dollop of whipped topping.
15. Repeat with the remaining shortcakes and blackberry mixture.
16. Serve immediately.

Chocolate Eclaire Cake

Ingredients:

2 eggs
6 oz. cream cheese
2 packets Splenda
1/4 tsp cream of tartar
1 large package of vanilla pudding mix, sugar free
2 cups milk
1 tbsp. vanilla flavoring
1 tbsp. vanilla syrup
1 small package sugar-free chocolate pudding mix
1-1/2 cups milk

Directions:

1. Preheat oven to 300 degrees.
2. Grease a 9 X 13 inch baking pan.
3. In two separate mixing bowls, separate and place the yolk in one bowl and the white in another.
4. In the bowl with the white, add cream of tartar.
5. Whip at high speed or until very stiff peaks form. In the bowl with the yolk, add cream cheese, 1/2 of the pudding mix, vanilla, sugar free syrup, and Splenda, and mix for 10 seconds, or until resembling runny scrambled eggs (you don't want a completely smooth batter).
6. Carefully fold the yolk into the whites.
7. Bake for 35 minutes.
8. While the batter is baking, make a pudding with 2 cups milk and the remaining pudding mix. Chill until set.
9. Make a second pudding with chocolate mix and only 1-1/2 cups milk. hill until set.
10. Once the cake base is removed from the oven, let cool.
11. Cut into thirds and place the first third in a loaf pan.
12. Layer 1/2 of the chilled pudding over the first layer. Follow with another slice of cake and the other half of the pudding. Finally, place the third oopsie layer on the top.
13. Over this, top with chocolate pudding layer.
14. Serve immediately, or keep chilled in the refrigerator.

Strawberry Shortcake

Sponge Cake Ingredients:

8 eggs, separated
8 oz. cream cheese
1 tsp vanilla extract
1/8 tsp cream of tartar
1/2 cup sugar substitute equivalent
1 scoop protein powder

Other Ingredients:

2 cups fresh strawberries, sliced + sweetener (see below)
Whipped topping recipe (below)

Cake Directions:

1. Whip the whites with cream of tartar until stiff peaks form, about 5 minutes.
2. In a separate bowl, combine cream cheese with egg yolks, vanilla extract, protein powder, sweetener and salt.
3. Gently fold the whites into the yolk mixture until combined.
4. Spread the oopsie batter evenly (this batter doesn't level out–it retains its shape, so if you leave it lump and bumpy, it's going to stay lumpy and bumpy) on the sheet cake covered with parchment paper (don't worry about greasing the pan or the parchment) and bake in a 300 degree oven for 30 minutes.
5. Let cool 15 minutes with a damp dish towel on top to keep cake from drying out.
6. Cut cake into 8 equal sections.
7. Set aside.

Strawberries Directions:

1. Soak in just enough water to almost cover the strawberries + 1/4 cup equivalent sugar substitute.
2. Let sit on counter for an hour or overnight in the refrigerator.

Cake Assembly Directions:

1. Place first cake layer on a plate
2. Top with whipped cream (recipe below).
3. Top with second cake, whipped cream and strawberries.

4. Serve cold. Leftover portions may be refrigerated, but are best stored separately and combined for service.

Whipped Topping

Ingredients:

1 cup heavy whipping cream
4 tbsp. sugar equivalent substitute (or more to taste)
1 tsp vanilla extract

Directions:

1. Whip all ingredients together ion high speed in a mixer until stiff peaks form.
2. Makes 4, double-layered shortcakes or 8 single layered shortcakes.

Caramel Cupcakes

Cake Ingredients:

1 cup almond flour
1 cup vanilla whey protein powder
1 tbsp. oat fiber
4 tbsp. Ideal Brown Sugar Sweetener
1 tbsp. baking powder
4 eggs
1 tsp. molasses
1 tsp. caramel flavor
1/2 tsp. vanilla extract
1/4 cup salted butter (1/2 a stick of butter), melted
1 cup unsweetened vanilla almond milk
Mix the dry ingredients.
Mix the wet ingredients in a separate bowl.
Mix all ingredients together.
Pour into muffin pan with butter spray.
Bake at 325 for 25-30 minutes.

Icing Ingredients:

1/4 cup of salted butter (1/2 stick)
1 tsp. of molasses
1 scoop of vanilla whey protein powder
4 tbsps. of Ideal Brown Sugar Sweetener
1 can of Nestle Table Cream
1 tsp. of caramel flavor

Directions:

1. Melt whey powder in butter in saucepan until smooth. Incorporate the rest of the ingredients, stirring until thoroughly heated.
2. Cool in the sauce pan, then refrigerate. Pipe onto the cupcake.

Coffee Crumb Cake

Batter Ingredients:

6 eggs, separated
6 oz. cream cheese, softened
1/2 cup sugar equivalent substitute
1/4 cup protein powder
1 tsp vanilla extract
1/4 tsp cream of tartar
1 tsp cinnamon

Crumb Topping Ingredients:

1 1/2 cups finely ground almond flour
2 tsp cinnamon
1/2 cup brown sugar equivalent substitute
1/2 stick (1/4 cup) cold butter, cubed

Glaze Ingredients:

1/2 cup heavy whipping cream
1 tbsp. sugar equivalent substitute
1 tsp cinnamon
2 tsp softened butter

Directions:

1. Preheat oven to 300 degrees F.
2. Prepare Oopsie batter:
3. Separate the egg yolks from the whites. Whip the whites with the cream of tartar until stiff peaks form.
4. Prepare other moist ingredients:
5. Beat the egg yolks with cream cheese, substitute sweetener, protein powder, vanilla extract, and cinnamon.
6. Fold this mixture with the eggs whites gently as not to deflate the whites.
7. Spoon mixture in an 8 inch square baking dish lined with parchment paper. You can also use an 8 inch spring form pan, generously greased with butter.
8. Set aside.
9. Prepare the crumb topping:

10. Place almond flour, brown sugar substitute, cinnamon and butter in a bowl and combine with your fingers (or a fork or pastry cutter) until well combined. It won't be crumbly, but it will hold together.
11. Add half of the crumb topping to the Oopsie batter evenly (it may sink to the bottom).
12. About half way through baking the cake, remove cake and add the remaining topping.
13. Continue baking. While the cake should bake for 40-50 minutes, Diana says to be sure to start testing the batter after 30 minutes with a toothpick to test for doneness (a clean toothpick), as some ovens cook hotter than others.

Glaze Directions:

1. Combine heavy cream, sweetener and cinnamon in a heat-proof measuring cup.
2. Heat in microwave or small sauce pan until sweetener has dissolved.
3. Mix well, adding butter and mix again. You can whip this to make it thicker when it's well chilled. Drizzle glaze on semi cooled crumb cake. Keep refrigerated.
4. This cake is best served the next day, even though it may be hard to resist. It gives the ingredients time to come together.

Boston Cream Napoleon

Ingredients:

3 eggs
3 oz. cream cheese
2 packets Splenda
1/8 tsp cream of tartar
pinch of salt
1 small sugar free instant French vanilla pudding
1 & 1/2 cups of 1% milk
1/3 cup heavy whipping cream
2 tbsps. sugar free chocolate syrup

Directions:

1. Preheat oven to 300 degrees F.
2. On high speed (with a mixer), mix whites with cream of tartar until stiff peaks form.
3. In a separate bowl, mix yolks with the Splenda, cream cheese, and added salt.
4. Combine yolk mixture by barely folding it in with the whites.
5. Bake in a medium-sized jelly roll pan on a silpat sprayed with Pam for 27 minutes at 300°.
6. Cooled.
7. Cut into 4 equal strips.
8. Mix pudding with milk, and layer like a Napoleon or Lasagna.
9. Mix whipping cream with 1 tbsp. of chocolate syrup and whip until frosting-like in thickness. Drizzle the top with the rest of the syrup. Chill for 4 hours.

Tiramisu

Ingredients:

1 cup heavy cream
1/4 cup granulated Stevia or other sugar substitute
8 oz mascarpone cheese, softened
1 tsp. vanilla extract
1/4 cup brewed espresso or strong coffee, cooled
1/4 cup unsweetened almond milk
1 package (about 7 oz) sugar-free ladyfingers
Unsweetened cocoa powder for dusting

Directions:

1. In a large mixing bowl, beat the heavy cream and sugar substitute with an electric mixer until stiff peaks form.
2. In a separate bowl, beat the mascarpone cheese, vanilla extract, brewed espresso or coffee, and almond milk until smooth.
3. Fold the whipped cream into the mascarpone mixture until well combined.
4. In a 9x13 inch baking dish, arrange a single layer of ladyfingers.
5. Spoon half of the mascarpone mixture over the ladyfingers and spread it evenly.
6. Repeat with another layer of ladyfingers and the remaining mascarpone mixture.
7. Cover and refrigerate for at least 2 hours or overnight.
8. Before serving, dust the top of the Tiramisu with unsweetened cocoa powder.

Pineapple Upside Down Cake

Ingredients:

1/4 cup butter or spectrum palm oil, softened (for batter).
1/4 cup butter or spectrum palm oil (for topping).
1/4 cup pure palm coconut palm sugar (low carb brown sugar for the topping).
1/2 cup heavy cream
5 large eggs
1 tsp. vanilla extract
2 cups almond flour (blanched almonds, ground in Nutribullet)
1 or 2 packets Stevia
1/2 cup of pineapple juice
1 can of pineapple slices (about 11 or 12)
12 dark mordello cherries

Directions:

1. Put 1/4 cup of butter or spectrum palm oil in a rectangular baking dish and melt it in a preheated oven at 350 degrees Fahrenheit.
2. Mix heavy cream, 1/4 cup butter or spectrum palm oil, eggs, vanilla, stevia, and almond flour in an electric mixer.
3. Beat on high until the batter looks fluffy and whipped. Then slowly add the pineapple juice.
4. When the batter is ready, take out the pan with the melted butter or palm oil.
5. Spread it around the pan evenly (without burning yourself).
6. Sprinkle 1/4 cup of the coconut palm sugar evenly over the bottom of the baking dish. Now layer your 9-12 pineapple slices.
7. Make it pretty, however it fits. In the center of each pineapple slice you can place a cherry if you'd like. It's not necessary. Then pour the batter on top. It will barely cover the pineapple slices and cherries. That's just fine.
8. Bake at 350 Fahrenheit for 35-45 minutes. Just watch it carefully to see how it is browning.
9. When it is nice and brown it's ready to come out of the oven.

Vanilla Coconut Cake

Ingredients:

2 cups almond flour
1/4 cup coconut flour
1/4 cup unsweetened shredded coconut
1/4 cup granulated Stevia or other sugar substitute
1 tsp. baking powder
1/2 tsp. baking soda
1/2 tsp. salt
4 eggs
1/4 cup coconut oil, melted
1/4 cup unsweetened almond milk
1 tsp. vanilla extract

Directions:

1. Preheat your oven to 350 degrees F (180°C).
2. Grease a 9-inch cake pan with cooking spray or coconut oil.
3. In a large mixing bowl, whisk together the almond flour, coconut flour, shredded coconut, sugar substitute, baking powder, baking soda, and salt.
4. In a separate bowl, whisk together the eggs, melted coconut oil, almond milk, and vanilla extract.
5. Add the wet ingredients to the dry ingredients and mix until well combined.
6. Pour the batter into the prepared cake pan and bake for 25-30 minutes or until a toothpick inserted into the center of the cake comes out clean.
7. Remove from the oven and let cool in the pan for 10 minutes.
8. Remove the cake from the pan and let it cool completely on a wire rack.
9. Frost the cake with sugar-free frosting or whipped cream, if desired.

Chocolate Pudding Cake

Ingredients:
1 cup almond flour
1/2 cup unsweetened cocoa powder
1/2 cup granulated Stevia or other sugar substitute
1 tsp. baking powder
1/2 tsp. baking soda
1/4 tsp. salt
1/2 cup unsweetened almond milk
1/4 cup coconut oil, melted
2 eggs
1 tsp. vanilla extract
1/2 cup hot water

Directions:
1. Preheat your oven to 350 degrees F (180°C).
2. Grease an 8-inch square baking dish with cooking spray or coconut oil.
3. In a large mixing bowl, whisk together the almond flour, cocoa powder, sugar substitute, baking powder, baking soda, and salt.
4. In a separate bowl, whisk together the almond milk, melted coconut oil, eggs, and vanilla extract.
5. Add the wet ingredients to the dry ingredients and mix until well combined.
6. Pour the batter into the prepared baking dish.
7. Sprinkle the top of the batter with the remaining sugar substitute.
8. Pour the hot water over the top of the batter, being careful not to stir.
9. Bake for 30-35 minutes or until a toothpick inserted into the center of the cake comes out clean.
10. Remove from the oven and let cool for 10 minutes.
11. Serve warm with sugar-free whipped cream or a sprinkle of cocoa powder, if desired.

Gingerbread Cupcakes

Ingredients:
1 1/2 cups almond flour
1/4 cup coconut flour
1/4 cup granulated Stevia or other sugar substitute
1 tsp. baking powder
1/2 tsp. baking soda
1/4 tsp. salt
1 tbsp. ground ginger
1 tsp. ground cinnamon
1/4 tsp. ground nutmeg
1/4 tsp. ground cloves
1/4 cup molasses
1/4 cup coconut oil, melted
1/4 cup unsweetened almond milk
2 eggs
1 tsp. vanilla extract

Directions:
1. Preheat your oven to 350 degrees F (180°C).
2. Line a muffin tin with paper liners.
3. In a large mixing bowl, whisk together the almond flour, coconut flour, sugar substitute, baking powder, baking soda, salt, ginger, cinnamon, nutmeg, and cloves.
4. In a separate bowl, whisk together the molasses, melted coconut oil, almond milk, eggs, and vanilla extract.
5. Add the wet ingredients to the dry ingredients and mix until well combined.
6. Spoon the batter into the prepared muffin tin, filling each cup about 2/3 full.
7. Bake for 18-20 minutes or until a toothpick inserted into the center of a cupcake comes out clean.
8. Remove from the oven and let cool in the muffin tin for 5 minutes.
9. Remove the cupcakes from the muffin tin and let cool completely on a wire rack.
10. Frost the cupcakes with sugar-free cream cheese frosting or whipped cream, if desired.

Pumpkin Spice Cake

Ingredients:

2 cups almond flour
1/2 cup coconut flour
1/4 cup granulated Stevia or other sugar substitute
2 tsps. baking powder
1 tsp. baking soda
1/2 tsp. salt
2 tsps. ground cinnamon
1/2 tsp. ground ginger
1/4 tsp. ground nutmeg
1/4 tsp. ground cloves
1 cup canned pumpkin puree
1/2 cup coconut oil, melted
1/4 cup unsweetened almond milk
3 eggs
1 tsp. vanilla extract

Directions:

1. Preheat your oven to 350 degrees F (180°C).
2. Grease a 9-inch cake pan with cooking spray or coconut oil.
3. In a large mixing bowl, whisk together the almond flour, coconut flour, sugar substitute, baking powder, baking soda, salt, cinnamon, ginger, nutmeg, and cloves.
4. In a separate bowl, whisk together the pumpkin puree, melted coconut oil, almond milk, eggs, and vanilla extract.
5. Add the wet ingredients to the dry ingredients and mix until well combined.
6. Pour the batter into the prepared cake pan.
7. Bake for 35-40 minutes or until a toothpick inserted into the center of the cake comes out clean.
8. Remove from the oven and let cool in the pan for 10 minutes.
9. Remove the cake from the pan and let it cool completely on a wire rack.
10. Frost the cake with sugar-free cream cheese frosting or whipped cream, if desired.

Almond Cake

Ingredients:

1 1/2 cups almond flour
1/2 cup granulated Stevia or other sugar substitute
1/2 tsp. baking powder
1/4 tsp. salt
1/4 cup coconut oil, melted
1/4 cup unsweetened almond milk
3 eggs
1 tsp. vanilla extract
1/4 tsp. almond extract
Optional: sliced almonds and/or powdered sugar substitute for topping

Directions:

1. Preheat your oven to 350 degrees F (180°C).
2. Grease an 8-inch cake pan with cooking spray or coconut oil.
3. In a large mixing bowl, whisk together the almond flour, sugar substitute, baking powder, and salt.
4. In a separate bowl, whisk together the melted coconut oil, almond milk, eggs, vanilla extract, and almond extract.
5. Add the wet ingredients to the dry ingredients and mix until well combined.
6. Pour the batter into the prepared cake pan.
7. Bake for 25-30 minutes or until a toothpick inserted into the center of the cake comes out clean.
8. Remove from the oven and let cool in the pan for 5 minutes.
9. Remove the cake from the pan and let it cool completely on a wire rack.
10. If desired, top the cake with sliced almonds and/or sprinkle with powdered sugar substitute.

Berry Sponge Cake

Ingredients:

4 eggs, separated
1/4 cup granulated sweetener (such as Stevia)
1/4 cup all-purpose flour
1/4 cup almond flour
1 tsp baking powder
1/4 tsp salt
1 tsp vanilla extract
1 cup mixed berries (such as strawberries, raspberries, and blueberries)
1 tbsp lemon juice

Directions:

1. Preheat the oven to 350 degrees F.
2. In a mixing bowl, beat the egg whites until stiff peaks form.
3. In a separate bowl, beat the egg yolks and sweetener together until light and fluffy.
4. In another bowl, mix together the all-purpose flour, almond flour, baking powder, and salt.
5. Add the flour mixture to the egg yolk mixture and stir until just combined.
6. Gently fold in the beaten egg whites until no white streaks remain.
7. Stir in the vanilla extract.
8. Pour the batter into a greased 8-inch cake pan.
9. Bake for 20-25 minutes or until a toothpick inserted into the center of the cake comes out clean.
10. While the cake is baking, prepare the berry topping.
11. In a saucepan, combine the mixed berries and lemon juice.
12. Cook over low heat until the berries have softened and released their juices.
13. Once the cake is done, remove it from the oven and let it cool for a few minutes.
14. Spoon the berry topping over the cake and serve.

Angel Food Cake

Ingredients:
1 cup all-purpose flour
1/4 cup cornstarch
1 1/2 cups granulated sweetener (such as Stevia)
12 egg whites, room temperature
1 1/2 tsp cream of tartar
1 tsp vanilla extract
1/4 tsp salt

Directions:
1. Preheat the oven to 350 degrees F.
2. In a mixing bowl, sift together the all-purpose flour and cornstarch.
3. In a separate mixing bowl, beat the egg whites until foamy.
4. Add the cream of tartar, vanilla extract, and salt to the egg whites and continue to beat until stiff peaks form.
5. Gradually add the granulated sweetener to the egg whites, about 1/4 cup at a time, while continuing to beat.
6. Gently fold in the flour mixture, about 1/4 cup at a time, until well combined.
7. Pour the batter into an ungreased 10-inch tube pan.
8. Bake for 35-40 minutes or until a toothpick inserted into the center of the cake comes out clean.
9. Remove from the oven and invert the pan onto a cooling rack.
10. Let the cake cool completely in the pan before removing it.
11. Run a knife around the edges of the cake and the center tube to release it from the pan.
12. Serve sliced with fresh berries or whipped cream, if desired.

Peach Cake

Ingredients:
1 1/2 cups all-purpose flour
1/2 cup almond flour
1 tsp baking powder
1/2 tsp baking soda
1/4 tsp salt
1/2 cup unsalted butter, softened
1/2 cup granulated sugar substitute (such as Stevia or Splenda)
2 large eggs
1/2 cup unsweetened applesauce
1/2 cup plain Greek yogurt
1 tsp vanilla extract
2 cups fresh or frozen peach slices, peeled and pitted
1 tbsp lemon juice

Directions:
1. Preheat the oven to 350 degrees F (175°C).
2. Grease a 9-inch cake pan with nonstick cooking spray.
3. In a medium bowl, whisk together the all-purpose flour, almond flour, baking powder, baking soda, and salt.
4. In a large bowl, cream together the butter and sugar substitute until light and fluffy.
5. Add the eggs, one at a time, beating well after each addition.
6. Add the applesauce, Greek yogurt, and vanilla extract to the butter mixture and beat until well combined.
7. Gradually add the flour mixture to the butter mixture, beating until just combined.
8. In a separate bowl, toss the peach slices with the lemon juice.
9. Spoon half of the cake batter into the prepared pan.
10. Arrange the peach slices on top of the batter in a single layer. Spoon the remaining batter over the peaches, spreading it evenly to cover.
11. Bake for 40-45 minutes, or until a toothpick inserted in the center comes out clean.
12. Let the cake cool in the pan for 10 minutes before transferring it to a wire rack to cool completely.

Little Italy Cake

Ingredients:
1 1/2 cups all-purpose flour
1/2 cup almond flour
1 tsp baking powder
1/2 tsp baking soda
1/4 tsp salt
1/2 cup unsalted butter, softened
1/2 cup granulated sugar substitute (such as Stevia or Splenda)
2 large eggs
1/2 cup unsweetened applesauce
1/2 cup plain Greek yogurt
1 tsp vanilla extract
1/4 cup unsweetened cocoa powder
1/2 cup strong brewed coffee, cooled
1/4 cup chopped walnuts (optional)

Directions:
1. Preheat the oven to 350 degrees F (175°C).
2. Grease a 9-inch cake pan with nonstick cooking spray.
3. In a medium bowl, whisk together the all-purpose flour, almond flour, baking powder, baking soda, and salt.
4. In a large bowl, cream together the butter and sugar substitute until light and fluffy.
5. Add the eggs, one at a time, beating well after each addition.
6. Add the applesauce, Greek yogurt, and vanilla extract to the butter mixture and beat until well combined.
7. Gradually add the flour mixture to the butter mixture, beating until just combined.
8. In a small bowl, whisk together the cocoa powder and cooled coffee until smooth.
9. Add the cocoa mixture to the cake batter and beat until well combined.
10. Fold in the chopped walnuts, if using.
11. Spoon the cake batter into the prepared pan and smooth the top with a spatula.
12. Bake for 40-45 minutes, or until a toothpick inserted in the center comes out clean.

13. Let the cake cool in the pan for 10 minutes before transferring it to a wire rack to cool completely.

Carrot Cake

Ingredients:

2 cups grated carrots
1 cup almond flour
1/2 cup coconut flour
1 tsp baking powder
1/2 tsp baking soda
1 tsp cinnamon
1/2 tsp nutmeg
1/2 tsp salt
4 eggs
1/2 cup unsweetened applesauce
1/4 cup coconut oil, melted
1/4 cup honey
1 tsp vanilla extract
1/2 cup chopped walnuts (optional)

Directions:

1. Preheat oven to 350°F (175°C) and grease a 9-inch cake pan.
2. In a large bowl, mix together the grated carrots, almond flour, coconut flour, baking powder, baking soda, cinnamon, nutmeg, and salt.
3. In a separate bowl, whisk together the eggs, applesauce, melted coconut oil, honey, and vanilla extract.
4. Add the wet ingredients to the dry ingredients and mix until well combined.
5. Fold in the chopped walnuts, if using.
6. Pour the batter into the prepared cake pan and smooth the top with a spatula.
7. Bake for 35-40 minutes, or until a toothpick inserted into the center comes out clean.
8. Let the cake cool in the pan for 10 minutes, then transfer it to a wire rack to cool completely.
9. Once the cake is cool, you can frost it with a diabetic-friendly cream cheese frosting, if desired.

Red Velvet Cake

Ingredients:
Red Velvet Cake
1 cup almond flour
1/2 cup coconut flour
1/2 cup unsweetened cocoa powder
1 tsp baking soda
1/2 tsp baking powder
1/4 tsp salt
4 eggs
1/2 cup unsweetened applesauce
1/4 cup coconut oil, melted
1/4 cup honey
1 tsp vanilla extract
1 tbsp red food coloring
1/2 cup low-fat buttermilk
1 tsp vinegar

Directions:
1. Preheat oven to 350°F (175°C) and grease a 9-inch cake pan.
2. In a large bowl, mix together the almond flour, coconut flour, cocoa powder, baking soda, baking powder, and salt.
3. In a separate bowl, whisk together the eggs, applesauce, melted coconut oil, honey, vanilla extract, and red food coloring.
4. Add the wet ingredients to the dry ingredients and mix until well combined.
5. In a small bowl, mix together the buttermilk and vinegar.
6. Add the buttermilk mixture to the cake batter and mix until well combined.
7. Pour the batter into the prepared cake pan and smooth the top with a spatula.
8. Bake for 35-40 minutes, or until a toothpick inserted into the center comes out clean.
9. Let the cake cool in the pan for 10 minutes, then transfer it to a wire rack to cool completely.
10. Once the cake is cool, you can frost it with a diabetic-friendly cream cheese frosting, if desired.

Vanilla Pound Cake

Ingredients:
1 1/2 cups almond flour
1/2 cup coconut flour
1/2 cup unsalted butter, softened
1 cup sugar substitute (such as erythritol or stevia)
4 large eggs
1/2 cup unsweetened almond milk
1 tbsp vanilla extract
1 tsp baking powder
1/4 tsp salt

Directions:
1. Preheat your oven to 350 degrees F (180°C).
2. Grease a 9x5 inch (23x13 cm) loaf pan with cooking spray.
3. In a large mixing bowl, beat the softened butter with a mixer until light and fluffy.
4. Add the sugar substitute to the butter and beat until well combined.
5. Add the eggs one at a time, beating well after each addition.
6. Stir in the almond flour, coconut flour, baking powder, and salt until well combined.
7. Add the almond milk and vanilla extract and mix until smooth.
8. Pour the batter into the prepared loaf pan and smooth out the top with a spatula.
9. Bake for 45-50 minutes or until a toothpick inserted into the center of the cake comes out clean.
10. Let the cake cool in the pan for 10 minutes before transferring it to a wire rack to cool completely.
11. Once cooled, slice and serve as desired.

Key Lime Cake

Ingredients:

1 1/2 cups all-purpose flour
1/2 cup almond flour
1/4 cup unsalted butter, softened
1/4 cup vegetable oil
1 cup granulated stevia sweetener
2 large eggs
1/4 cup fresh lime juice
1 tbsp. lime zest
1/2 cup unsweetened almond milk
1 tsp. baking powder
1/2 tsp. baking soda
1/4 tsp. salt

Icing Ingredients:

1 cup powdered stevia sweetener
1/4 cup fresh lime juice
1 tbsp. lime zest
1 tbsp. unsalted butter, softened
1/4 cup fat-free Greek yogurt

Directions:

1. Preheat the oven to 350 degrees F (180°C).
2. Grease a 9-inch cake pan with cooking spray.
3. In a large mixing bowl, cream together the softened butter, vegetable oil, and granulated stevia sweetener until light and fluffy.
4. Add the eggs, one at a time, beating well after each addition.
5. Add the lime juice and lime zest, and mix well.
6. In a separate bowl, whisk together the all-purpose flour, almond flour, baking powder, baking soda, and salt.
7. Add the dry ingredients to the wet ingredients, alternating with the almond milk, beginning and ending with the dry ingredients.
8. Mix until just combined.
9. Pour the batter into the prepared cake pan and smooth the top.

10. Bake for 25-30 minutes, or until a toothpick inserted into the center of the cake comes out clean.
11. While the cake is baking, prepare the icing.
12. In a small bowl, whisk together the powdered stevia sweetener, lime juice, lime zest, and softened butter until smooth.
13. Add the Greek yogurt and whisk until well combined.
14. Once the cake has cooled, spread the icing over the top of the cake.
15. Serve and enjoy!

Yellow Cake

Ingredients:
1 1/2 cups all-purpose flour
1 cup granulated stevia sweetener
1/4 cup unsalted butter, softened
1/4 cup vegetable oil
2 large eggs
1/2 cup unsweetened almond milk
1 tsp. baking powder
1/2 tsp. baking soda
1/4 tsp. salt
1 tsp. vanilla extract

Directions:
1. Preheat the oven to 350 degrees F (180°C).
2. Grease an 8-inch cake pan with cooking spray.
3. In a large mixing bowl, cream together the softened butter, vegetable oil, and granulated stevia sweetener until light and fluffy.
4. Add the eggs, one at a time, beating well after each addition.
5. Add the vanilla extract, and mix well.
6. In a separate bowl, whisk together the all-purpose flour, baking powder, baking soda, and salt.
7. Add the dry ingredients to the wet ingredients, alternating with the almond milk, beginning and ending with the dry ingredients.
8. Mix until just combined.
9. Pour the batter into the prepared cake pan and smooth the top.
10. Bake for 25-30 minutes, or until a toothpick inserted into the center of the cake comes out clean.
11. Let the cake cool in the pan for 5 minutes before transferring it to a wire rack to cool completely.
12. Once the cake has cooled, serve and enjoy!

Hummingbird Cake:

Ingredients:

1 1/2 cups all-purpose flour
1/2 cup almond flour
1 cup granulated stevia sweetener
1 tsp. baking powder
1/2 tsp. baking soda
1/4 tsp. salt
1 tsp. ground cinnamon
1/4 cup unsalted butter, softened
1/4 cup vegetable oil
2 large eggs
1/2 cup unsweetened applesauce
1/2 cup crushed pineapple, drained
1/2 cup mashed ripe bananas
1/2 cup chopped pecans
1 tsp. vanilla extract

Frosting Ingredients:

1/2 cup powdered stevia sweetener
1/4 cup fat-free cream cheese, softened
1/2 tsp. vanilla extract

Directions:

1. Preheat the oven to 350 degrees F (180°C).
2. Grease a 9-inch cake pan with cooking spray.
3. In a large mixing bowl, whisk together the all-purpose flour, almond flour, granulated stevia sweetener, baking powder, baking soda, salt, and ground cinnamon.
4. In a separate bowl, cream together the softened butter, vegetable oil, and eggs until light and fluffy.
5. Add the mashed bananas, crushed pineapple, and unsweetened applesauce, and mix well.
6. Gradually add the dry ingredients to the wet ingredients, mixing until just combined.
7. Fold in the chopped pecans and vanilla extract.
8. Pour the batter into the prepared cake pan and smooth the top.

9. Bake for 30-35 minutes, or until a toothpick inserted into the center of the cake comes out clean.
10. Let the cake cool in the pan for 5 minutes before transferring it to a wire rack to cool completely.
11. While the cake is cooling, prepare the frosting.
12. In a medium bowl, whisk together the powdered stevia sweetener, softened cream cheese, and vanilla extract until smooth.
13. Once the cake has cooled, spread the frosting over the top of the cake.
14. Serve and enjoy!

Diabetic Lemon Cake

Ingredients:

1 cup all-purpose flour
1/2 cup granulated sugar substitute
1/2 cup unsweetened applesauce
1/4 cup vegetable oil
1/4 cup low-fat milk
2 tsps. baking powder
1 tsp. lemon zest
1/2 tsp. salt
2 large eggs
1/4 cup freshly squeezed lemon juice

Directions:

1. Preheat the oven to 350 degrees F.
2. Grease a 9-inch cake pan.
3. In a large bowl, whisk together the flour, sugar substitute, baking powder, lemon zest, and salt.
4. In a separate bowl, whisk together the applesauce, oil, milk, eggs, and lemon juice.
5. Add the wet ingredients to the dry ingredients and stir until just combined.
6. Pour the batter into the prepared cake pan and bake for 25-30 minutes or until a toothpick inserted into the center comes out clean.
7. Let cool before serving.

Diabetic Banana Cake

Ingredients:

1 cup all-purpose flour
1/2 cup granulated sugar substitute
1/2 cup unsweetened applesauce
1/4 cup vegetable oil
1/4 cup low-fat milk
2 tsps. baking powder
1/2 tsps. ground cinnamon
1/2 tsp. salt
2 large ripe bananas, mashed

Directions:

1. Preheat the oven to 350 degrees F.
2. Grease a 9-inch cake pan.
3. In a large bowl, whisk together the flour, sugar substitute, baking powder, cinnamon, and salt.
4. In a separate bowl, whisk together the applesauce, oil, milk, eggs, and mashed bananas.
5. Add the wet ingredients to the dry ingredients and stir until just combined.
6. Pour the batter into the prepared cake pan and bake for 25-30 minutes or until a toothpick inserted into the center comes out clean.
7. Let cool before serving.

Diabetic Vanilla Cake

Ingredients:

1 cup all-purpose flour
1/2 cup granulated sugar substitute
1/2 cup unsweetened applesauce
1/4 cup vegetable oil
1/4 cup low-fat milk
2 tsps. baking powder
1 tsp. vanilla extract
1/2 tsp. salt
2 large eggs

Directions:

1. Preheat the oven to 350 degrees F.
2. Grease a 9-inch cake pan.
3. In a large bowl, whisk together the flour, sugar substitute, baking powder, and salt.
4. In a separate bowl, whisk together the applesauce, oil, milk, eggs, and vanilla extract.
5. Add the wet ingredients to the dry ingredients and stir until just combined.
6. Pour the batter into the prepared cake pan and bake for 25-30 minutes or until a toothpick inserted into the center comes out clean.
7. Let cool before serving.

Blueberry Coffee Cake

Ingredients:

1 1/2 cups almond flour
1/4 cup coconut flour
1/4 cup unsweetened applesauce
1/4 cup coconut oil, melted
1/4 cup honey or maple syrup
3 large eggs
1 tsp. baking powder
1/2 tsp. baking soda
1/4 tsp. salt
1 tsp. vanilla extract
1 cup fresh blueberries
1/4 cup chopped walnuts (optional)

Directions:

1. Preheat the oven to 350 degrees F (175°C).
2. Grease a 9-inch cake pan with coconut oil.
3. In a large mixing bowl, whisk together the almond flour, coconut flour, baking powder, baking soda, and salt.
4. In another mixing bowl, mix together the applesauce, coconut oil, honey/maple syrup, eggs, and vanilla extract until well combined.
5. Add the wet ingredients to the dry ingredients and mix until well combined.
6. Fold in the fresh blueberries and chopped walnuts (if using).
7. Pour the batter into the prepared cake pan and bake for 25-30 minutes or until a toothpick comes out clean.
8. Let the cake cool before slicing and serving.

Apple Cinnamon Diabetic Cake

Ingredients:

2 cups almond flour
1/4 cup coconut flour
1 tsp baking powder
1 tsp cinnamon
1/4 tsp salt
1/4 cup coconut oil, melted
1/4 cup honey or maple syrup
3 large eggs
1/4 cup unsweetened almond milk
2 cups diced apples

Directions:

1. Preheat oven to 350 degrees F (180°C).
2. Grease an 8-inch cake pan.
3. In a large bowl, whisk together almond flour, coconut flour, baking powder, cinnamon, and salt.
4. In another bowl, whisk together melted coconut oil, honey or maple syrup, eggs, almond milk.
5. Pour wet ingredients into dry ingredients and mix well.
6. Fold in diced apples.
7. Pour batter into the prepared pan and bake for 30-35 minutes or until a toothpick inserted in the center comes out clean.

Lemon Poppy Seed Cake

Ingredients:

2 cups almond flour
1/2 cup coconut flour
1 tsp baking powder
1/2 tsp baking soda
1/4 tsp salt
1/4 cup coconut oil, melted
1/4 cup honey or maple syrup
3 large eggs
1/4 cup unsweetened almond milk
1/4 cup fresh lemon juice
1 tbsp lemon zest
2 tbsp poppy seeds

Directions:

1. Preheat oven to 350 degrees F (180°C).
2. Grease an 8-inch cake pan.
3. In a large bowl, whisk together almond flour, coconut flour, baking powder, baking soda, and salt.
4. In another bowl, whisk together melted coconut oil, honey or maple syrup, eggs, almond milk, lemon juice, and lemon zest.
5. Pour wet ingredients into dry ingredients and mix well.
6. Fold in poppy seeds.
7. Pour batter into the prepared pan and bake for 25-30 minutes or until a toothpick inserted in the center comes out clean.

Almond Flour Coffee Cake

Ingredients:

2 cups almond flour
1/2 cup coconut flour
1 tsp baking powder
1/2 tsp baking soda
1/4 tsp salt
1/4 cup coconut oil, melted
1/4 cup honey or maple syrup
3 large eggs
1/4 cup unsweetened almond milk
1 tsp vanilla extract
1/4 cup chopped pecans (optional)

Directions:

1. Preheat oven to 350 degrees F (180°C).
2. Grease an 8-inch cake pan.
3. In a large bowl, whisk together almond flour, coconut flour, baking powder, baking soda, and salt.
4. In another bowl, whisk together melted coconut oil, honey or maple syrup, eggs, almond milk, and vanilla extract.
5. Pour wet ingredients into dry ingredients and mix well.
6. Fold in chopped pecans, if using.
7. Pour batter into the prepared pan and bake for 25-30 minutes or until a toothpick inserted in the center comes out clean.

Peanut Butter Chocolate Chip Cake

Ingredients:
2 cups almond flour
1/2 cup coconut flour
1 tsp baking powder
1/2 tsp baking soda
1/4 tsp salt
1/2 cup creamy peanut butter
1/4 cup honey or maple syrup
3 large eggs
1/4 cup unsweetened almond milk
1 tsp vanilla extract
1/2 cup sugar-free chocolate chips

Directions:
1. Preheat oven to 350 degrees F (180°C).
2. Grease an 8-inch cake pan.
3. In a large bowl, whisk together almond flour, coconut flour, baking powder, baking soda, and salt.
4. In another bowl, whisk together peanut butter, honey or maple syrup, eggs, almond milk, and vanilla extract.
5. Pour wet ingredients into dry ingredients and mix well.
6. Fold in chocolate chips.
7. Pour batter into the prepared pan and bake for 25-30 minutes or until a toothpick inserted in the center comes out clean.

Raspberry Coconut Cake

Ingredients:

2 cups almond flour
1/2 cup coconut flour
1 tsp baking powder
1/2 tsp baking soda
1/4 tsp salt
1/4 cup coconut oil, melted
1/4 cup granulated sweetener (such as erythritol or stevia)
3 large eggs
1/4 cup unsweetened almond milk
1 tsp vanilla extract
1 cup fresh or frozen raspberries
1/2 cup shredded coconut

Directions:

1. Preheat oven to 350 degrees F (180°C).
2. Grease an 8-inch cake pan.
3. In a large bowl, whisk together almond flour, coconut flour, baking powder, baking soda, and salt.
4. In another bowl, whisk together melted coconut oil, sweetener, eggs, almond milk, and vanilla extract.
5. Pour wet ingredients into dry ingredients and mix well.
6. Fold in raspberries and shredded coconut.
7. Pour batter into the prepared pan and bake for 25-30 minutes or until a toothpick inserted in the center comes out clean.
8. Let the cake cool for a few minutes before slicing and serving. Enjoy!

Chocolate Zucchini Cake

Ingredients:

2 cups almond flour
1/2 cup coconut flour
1/2 cup cocoa powder
1 tsp baking powder
1/2 tsp baking soda
1/4 tsp salt
1/4 cup coconut oil, melted
1/4 cup granulated sweetener (such as erythritol or stevia)
3 large eggs
1/4 cup unsweetened almond milk
1 tsp vanilla extract
2 cups grated zucchini

Directions:

1. Preheat oven to 350 degrees F (180°C).
2. Grease an 8-inch cake pan.
3. In a large bowl, whisk together almond flour, coconut flour, cocoa powder, baking powder, baking soda, and salt.
4. In another bowl, whisk together melted coconut oil, sweetener, eggs, almond milk, and vanilla extract.
5. Pour wet ingredients into dry ingredients and mix well.
6. Fold in grated zucchini.
7. Pour batter into the prepared pan and bake for 25-30 minutes or until a toothpick inserted in the center comes out clean.

Chocolate Almond Cake

Ingredients:

2 cups almond flour
1/2 cup cocoa powder
1 tsp baking powder
1/2 tsp baking soda
1/4 tsp salt
1/4 cup coconut oil, melted
1/4 cup granulated sweetener (such as erythritol or stevia)
3 large eggs
1/4 cup unsweetened almond milk
1 tsp vanilla extract
1/4 cup sliced almonds

Directions:

1. Preheat oven to 350 degrees F (180°C).
2. Grease an 8-inch cake pan.
3. In a large bowl, whisk together almond flour, cocoa powder, baking powder, baking soda, and salt.
4. In another bowl, whisk together melted coconut oil, sweetener, eggs, almond milk, and vanilla extract.
5. Pour wet ingredients into dry ingredients and mix well.
6. Fold in sliced almonds.
7. Pour batter into the prepared pan and bake for 25-30 minutes or until a toothpick inserted in the center comes out clean.

Cherry Almond Cake

Ingredients:

1/2 cup unsalted butter, softened
1/2 cup granulated erythritol
2 large eggs
1 tsp. almond extract
1 1/2 cups almond flour
1/2 tsp. baking soda
1/4 tsp. salt
1/2 cup unsweetened almond milk
1/2 cup fresh or frozen pitted cherries, chopped

Directions:

1. Preheat the oven to 350 degrees F (175°C).
2. Grease a 9-inch cake pan with cooking spray or butter.
3. In a large mixing bowl, cream together the softened butter and erythritol until light and fluffy.
4. Add in the eggs one at a time, beating well after each addition.
5. Mix in the almond extract.
6. In a separate bowl, whisk together the almond flour, baking soda, and salt.
7. Gradually mix the dry ingredients into the wet mixture until just combined.
8. Pour in the almond milk and mix until the batter is smooth.
9. Fold in the chopped cherries.
10. Pour the batter into the prepared cake pan and smooth the top with a spatula.
11. Bake for 25-30 minutes, or until a toothpick inserted into the center of the cake comes out clean.
12. Allow the cake to cool in the pan for 10 minutes, then transfer it to a wire rack to cool completely.
13. Serve the cake with fresh cherries on top if desired.

Apricot Almond Cake

Ingredients:

1/2 cup unsalted butter, softened
1/2 cup granulated erythritol
2 large eggs
1 tsp. almond extract
1 1/2 cups almond flour
1/2 tsp. baking soda
1/4 tsp. salt
1/2 cup unsweetened almond milk
1/2 cup chopped dried apricots
1/2 cup slivered almonds

Directions:

1. Preheat the oven to 350 degrees F (175°C).
2. Grease a 9-inch cake pan with cooking spray or butter.
3. In a large mixing bowl, cream together the softened butter and erythritol until light and fluffy.
4. Add in the eggs one at a time, beating well after each addition.
5. Mix in the almond extract.
6. In a separate bowl, whisk together the almond flour, baking soda, and salt.
7. Gradually mix the dry ingredients into the wet mixture until just combined.
8. Pour in the almond milk and mix until the batter is smooth.
9. Fold in the chopped dried apricots and slivered almonds.
10. Pour the batter into the prepared cake pan and smooth the top with a spatula.
11. Bake for 25-30 minutes, or until a toothpick inserted into the center of the cake comes out clean.
12. Allow the cake to cool in the pan for 10 minutes, then transfer it to a wire rack to cool completely.
13. Serve the cake with additional chopped apricots and slivered almonds on top if desired.

Black Forest Cake

Cake Ingredients:

2 cups almond flour
1/2 cup unsweetened cocoa powder
1/2 cup granulated erythritol
1/4 cup coconut flour
1 tbsp. baking powder
1/2 tsp. salt
4 large eggs
1/2 cup unsweetened almond milk
1/4 cup coconut oil, melted
1 tsp. vanilla extract

Filling and Frosting Ingredients:

1 can (14 oz.) pitted cherries, drained
1 cup heavy whipping cream
1/4 cup powdered erythritol
1 tsp. vanilla extract

Directions:

1. Preheat the oven to 350 degrees F (175°C).
2. Grease two 9-inch round cake pans with cooking spray or butter.
3. In a large mixing bowl, whisk together the almond flour, cocoa powder, erythritol, coconut flour, baking powder, and salt.
4. In a separate bowl, whisk together the eggs, almond milk, melted coconut oil, and vanilla extract.
5. Gradually mix the wet ingredients into the dry mixture until just combined.
6. Divide the batter evenly between the two prepared cake pans.
7. Bake for 20-25 minutes, or until a toothpick inserted into the center of the cakes comes out clean.
8. Allow the cakes to cool in the pans for 10 minutes, then transfer them to wire racks to cool completely.

Filling and Frosting Directions:

1. In a large mixing bowl, beat the heavy cream with an electric mixer on high speed until soft peaks form.

2. Add in the powdered erythritol and vanilla extract, and continue to beat until stiff peaks form.
3. On a cake plate or stand, place one of the cooled cake layers.
4. Top the cake layer with a layer of whipped cream, spreading it evenly.
5. Add the drained cherries on top of the whipped cream layer.
6. Place the second cake layer on top of the cherries.
7. Frost the top and sides of the cake with the remaining whipped cream.
8. Decorate the top of the cake with additional cherries and grated chocolate, if desired.

Chocolate Cherry Cake

Ingredients:

1 1/4 cups all-purpose flour
1/2 cup unsweetened cocoa powder
1 tsp baking powder
1/2 tsp baking soda
1/4 tsp salt
1/4 cup unsweetened applesauce
1/4 cup vegetable oil
1/2 cup granulated sugar substitute (such as stevia)
2 eggs
1 tsp vanilla extract
1/2 cup low-fat milk
1 cup frozen unsweetened cherries, thawed and chopped

Directions:

1. Preheat the oven to 350 degrees F (175°C) and grease a 9-inch cake pan.
2. In a medium bowl, whisk together the flour, cocoa powder, baking powder, baking soda, and salt.
3. In a separate large bowl, beat the applesauce, oil, and sugar substitute until well combined.
4. Add the eggs and vanilla extract to the large bowl and beat until smooth.
5. Gradually add the dry ingredients to the large bowl, alternating with the milk, and mix until just combined.
6. Fold in the chopped cherries.
7. Pour the batter into the greased cake pan and bake for 25-30 minutes, or until a toothpick inserted into the center of the cake comes out clean.
8. Allow the cake to cool in the pan for 10 minutes before transferring it to a wire rack to cool completely.
9. Serve and enjoy your delicious chocolate cherry cake!

Pistachio Cake

Ingredients:

1 1/4 cups all-purpose flour
1/4 cup cornstarch
2 tsp baking powder
1/2 tsp baking soda
1/2 tsp salt
1/2 cup unsalted butter, softened
1 cup granulated sugar substitute (such as stevia)
2 eggs
1 tsp vanilla extract
1/2 cup low-fat milk
1/2 cup unsalted pistachios, finely chopped
Green food coloring (optional)

Directions:

1. Preheat the oven to 350 degrees F (175°C) and grease a 9-inch cake pan.
2. In a medium bowl, whisk together the flour, cornstarch, baking powder, baking soda, and salt.
3. In a separate large bowl, beat the butter and sugar substitute until well combined.
4. Add the eggs and vanilla extract to the large bowl and beat until smooth.
5. Gradually add the dry ingredients to the large bowl, alternating with the milk, and mix until just combined.
6. Fold in the chopped pistachios and green food coloring (if desired).
7. Pour the batter into the greased cake pan and bake for 30-35 minutes, or until a toothpick inserted into the center of the cake comes out clean.
8. Allow the cake to cool in the pan for 10 minutes before transferring it to a wire rack to cool completely.

Cookies 'n' Cream Cupcakes

Ingredients:
1 1/2 cups all-purpose flour
1/2 cup unsweetened cocoa powder
1 tsp baking soda
1/2 tsp baking powder
1/2 tsp salt
1/2 cup unsweetened applesauce
1/4 cup vegetable oil
1/2 cup granulated sugar substitute (such as stevia)
2 eggs
1 tsp vanilla extract
1/2 cup low-fat milk
12 sugar-free chocolate sandwich cookies, crushed

Frosting Ingredients:
1/2 cup unsalted butter, softened
1/2 cup powdered sugar substitute (such as erythritol)
1 tsp vanilla extract
4 sugar-free chocolate sandwich cookies, crushed

Directions:
1. Preheat the oven to 350 degrees F (175°C) and line a muffin tin with 12 paper liners.
2. In a medium bowl, whisk together the flour, cocoa powder, baking soda, baking powder, and salt.
3. In a separate large bowl, beat the applesauce, oil, and sugar substitute until well combined.
4. Add the eggs and vanilla extract to the large bowl and beat until smooth.
5. Gradually add the dry ingredients to the large bowl, alternating with the milk, and mix until just combined.
6. Fold in the crushed chocolate sandwich cookies.
7. Pour the batter evenly into the lined muffin tin, filling each cup about 2/3 full.
8. Bake for 18-20 minutes, or until a toothpick inserted into the center of a cupcake comes out clean.
9. Allow the cupcakes to cool in the tin for 5 minutes before transferring them to a wire rack to cool completely.

10. To make the frosting, beat the butter, powdered sugar substitute, and vanilla extract in a large bowl until smooth and creamy.
11. Fold in the crushed chocolate sandwich cookies.
12. Frost the cooled cupcakes with the frosting and top with additional crushed cookies, if desired.

Orange Dream Angel Cake

Ingredients:
1 box (16 oz) angel food cake mix
1 can (11 oz) mandarin oranges in light syrup, drained
1 cup low-fat milk
1 package (1 oz) sugar-free vanilla instant pudding mix
1 tub (8 oz) light whipped topping, thawed
Orange zest, for garnish (optional)

Directions:
1. Preheat the oven to 350 degrees F (175°C) and prepare an angel food cake pan according to the package instructions.
2. In a large bowl, mix together the angel food cake mix and the mandarin oranges until well combined.
3. Pour the mixture into the prepared cake pan and bake for 35-40 minutes, or until the cake is golden brown and a toothpick inserted into the center comes out clean.
4. Allow the cake to cool in the pan upside down for at least an hour before removing it from the pan.
5. In a medium bowl, whisk together the milk and the sugar-free vanilla instant pudding mix until thickened.
6. Fold in the thawed whipped topping until well combined.
7. Slice the cooled cake horizontally into three layers.
8. Spread the pudding mixture between the layers and over the top of the cake.
9. Garnish with orange zest, if desired.

Diabetic Chocolate Cherry Cola Poke Cake

Ingredients:
1 cup almond flour
1/2 cup unsweetened cocoa powder
1/4 cup coconut flour
1 tsp baking powder
1/2 tsp baking soda
1/4 tsp salt
3/4 cup plain Greek yogurt
1/2 cup unsweetened almond milk
1/4 cup coconut oil, melted
3 large eggs
1 tsp vanilla extract
1/2 cup erythritol (or other low-calorie sweetener)
1 can of diet cherry cola
1/2 cup sugar-free cherry jam

Directions:
1. Preheat the oven to 350 degrees F (175°C) and grease a 9-inch cake pan with cooking spray.
2. In a large mixing bowl, whisk together the almond flour, cocoa powder, coconut flour, baking powder, baking soda, and salt.
3. In a separate mixing bowl, whisk together the Greek yogurt, almond milk, melted coconut oil, eggs, vanilla extract, and erythritol.
4. Gradually add the dry ingredients to the wet ingredients, whisking until the batter is smooth and well combined.
5. Pour the batter into the prepared cake pan and bake for 30-35 minutes or until a toothpick inserted into the center of the cake comes out clean.
6. Let the cake cool for 10-15 minutes, then poke holes all over the top of the cake with a fork.
7. Mix together the can of diet cherry cola and the sugar-free cherry jam, then pour the mixture over the cake, making sure it gets into all the holes.
8. Let the cake cool completely before slicing and serving.

Diabetic Oatmeal Coffee Cake

Ingredients:
1 cup almond flour
1/2 cup oat flour
1/2 cup rolled oats
1 tsp baking powder
1/2 tsp baking soda
1/4 tsp salt
3/4 cup plain Greek yogurt
1/2 cup unsweetened almond milk
1/4 cup coconut oil, melted
3 large eggs
1 tsp vanilla extract
1/2 cup erythritol (or other low calorie sweetener)
1/2 cup chopped walnuts
1 tsp ground cinnamon

Directions:
1. Preheat the oven to 350 degrees F (175°C) and grease a 9-inch cake pan with cooking spray.
2. In a large mixing bowl, whisk together the almond flour, oat flour, rolled oats, baking powder, baking soda, and salt.
3. In a separate mixing bowl, whisk together the Greek yogurt, almond milk, melted coconut oil, eggs, vanilla extract, and erythritol.
4. Gradually add the dry ingredients to the wet ingredients, whisking until the batter is smooth and well combined.
5. Fold in the chopped walnuts and ground cinnamon.
6. Pour the batter into the prepared cake pan and smooth out the top.
7. Bake for 30-35 minutes or until a toothpick inserted into the center of the cake comes out clean.
8. Let the cake cool completely before slicing and serving.

Diabetic Mocha Cake

Ingredients:

1 cup almond flour
1/2 cup oat flour
1/2 cup unsweetened cocoa powder
1 tsp baking powder
1/2 tsp baking soda
1/4 tsp salt
3/4 cup plain Greek yogurt
1/2 cup unsweetened almond milk
1/4 cup coconut oil, melted
3 large eggs
1 tsp vanilla extract
1/2 cup erythritol (or other low-calorie sweetener)
2 tbsp instant coffee granules
1/2 cup hot water

Directions:

1. Preheat the oven to 350 degrees F (175°C) and grease a 9-inch cake pan with cooking spray.
2. In a large mixing bowl, whisk together the almond flour, oat flour, cocoa powder, baking powder, baking soda, and salt.
3. In a separate mixing bowl, whisk together the Greek yogurt, almond milk, melted coconut oil, eggs, vanilla extract, and erythritol.
4. In a small bowl, dissolve the instant coffee granules in hot water and stir until completely dissolved.
5. Gradually add the dry ingredients to the wet ingredients, whisking until the batter is smooth and well combined.
6. Pour the coffee into the batter and mix until well combined.
7. Pour the batter into the prepared cake pan and bake for 30-35 minutes or until a toothpick inserted into the center of the cake comes out clean.
8. Let the cake cool completely before slicing and serving. Optional: top with a sugar-free frosting or whipped cream for added sweetness.

Diabetic Strawberry Cream Cake

Ingredients:
1 cup almond flour
1/2 cup oat flour
1 tsp baking powder
1/2 tsp baking soda
1/4 tsp salt
3/4 cup plain Greek yogurt
1/2 cup unsweetened almond milk
1/4 cup coconut oil, melted
3 large eggs
1 tsp vanilla extract
1/2 cup erythritol (or other low-calorie sweetener)
1 cup fresh strawberries, chopped
1/2 cup heavy whipping cream

Directions:
1. Preheat the oven to 350 degrees F (175°C) and grease a 9-inch cake pan with cooking spray.
2. In a large mixing bowl, whisk together the almond flour, oat flour, baking powder, baking soda, and salt.
3. In a separate mixing bowl, whisk together the Greek yogurt, almond milk, melted coconut oil, eggs, vanilla extract, and erythritol.
4. Gradually add the dry ingredients to the wet ingredients, whisking until the batter is smooth and well combined.
5. Fold in the chopped strawberries.
6. Pour the batter into the prepared cake pan and bake for 30-35 minutes or until a toothpick inserted into the center of the cake comes out clean.
7. Let the cake cool completely before slicing.
8. In a medium mixing bowl, whip the heavy whipping cream until stiff peaks form.
9. Spread the whipped cream over the top of the cake before serving.

Diabetic Cranberry Orange Cake

Ingredients:

1 cup almond flour
1/2 cup oat flour
1 tsp baking powder
1/2 tsp baking soda
1/4 tsp salt
3/4 cup plain Greek yogurt
1/2 cup unsweetened almond milk
1/4 cup coconut oil, melted
3 large eggs
1 tsp vanilla extract
1/2 cup erythritol (or other low-calorie sweetener)
1 cup fresh cranberries, chopped
1 tbsp orange zest

Directions:

1. Preheat the oven to 350 degrees F (175°C) and grease a 9-inch cake pan with cooking spray.
2. In a large mixing bowl, whisk together the almond flour, oat flour, baking powder, baking soda, and salt.
3. In a separate mixing bowl, whisk together the Greek yogurt, almond milk, melted coconut oil, eggs, vanilla extract, and erythritol.
4. Gradually add the dry ingredients to the wet ingredients, whisking until the batter is smooth and well combined.
5. Fold in the chopped cranberries and orange zest.
6. Pour the batter into the prepared cake pan and bake for 30-35 minutes or until a toothpick inserted into the center of the cake comes out clean.
7. Let the cake cool completely before slicing and serving.

Lemon Ricotta Cake

Ingredients:

1 1/2 cups almond flour
1/2 cup coconut flour
2 tsp baking powder
1/2 tsp baking soda
1/4 tsp salt
3/4 cup plain Greek yogurt
1/2 cup unsweetened almond milk
1/4 cup coconut oil, melted
3 large eggs
1 tsp vanilla extract
1/2 cup erythritol (or other low-calorie sweetener)
1/2 cup part-skim ricotta cheese
1/4 cup fresh lemon juice
1 tbsp lemon zest

Directions:

1. Preheat the oven to 350 degrees F (175°C) and grease a 9-inch cake pan with cooking spray.
2. In a large mixing bowl, whisk together the almond flour, coconut flour, baking powder, baking soda, and salt.
3. In a separate mixing bowl, whisk together the Greek yogurt, almond milk, melted coconut oil, eggs, vanilla extract, and erythritol.
4. Gradually add the dry ingredients to the wet ingredients, whisking until the batter is smooth and well combined.
5. Fold in the ricotta cheese, lemon juice, and lemon zest.
6. Pour the batter into the prepared cake pan and bake for 30-35 minutes or until a toothpick inserted into the center of the cake comes out clean.
7. Let the cake cool completely before slicing and serving.

Chocolate Chip Cheesecake Cupcakes

Ingredients:

8 oz reduced-fat cream cheese, softened
1/4 cup plain Greek yogurt
1/4 cup unsweetened almond milk
1/4 cup erythritol (or other low-calorie sweetener)
2 large eggs
1 tsp vanilla extract
1/4 cup mini chocolate chips
12 sugar-free vanilla wafer cookies

Directions:

1. Preheat the oven to 350 degrees F (175°C) and line a muffin tin with 12 paper liners.
2. In a mixing bowl, beat the cream cheese until smooth and creamy.
3. Add in the Greek yogurt, almond milk, and erythritol and beat until well combined.
4. Add in the eggs one at a time, beating well after each addition.
5. Stir in the vanilla extract and mini chocolate chips.
6. Place a vanilla wafer cookie in the bottom of each paper liner.
7. Pour the cheesecake mixture over the cookie, filling each liner about 3/4 full.
8. Bake for 20-25 minutes or until the cheesecake is set.
9. Remove the cupcakes from the oven and let them cool to room temperature.
10. Chill the cupcakes in the fridge for at least 30 minutes before serving.

Peanut Butter Lava Cupcakes

Ingredients:
1/2 cup natural peanut butter
1/4 cup unsweetened applesauce
1/4 cup erythritol (or other low-calorie sweetener)
2 large eggs
1/2 cup almond flour
1/4 cup unsweetened cocoa powder
1 tsp baking powder
1/4 tsp salt
1/4 cup unsweetened almond milk
Sugar-free dark chocolate chips, for filling

Dircctions:
1. Preheat the oven to 350 degrees F (175°C) and line a muffin tin with 6 paper liners.
2. In a mixing bowl, beat the peanut butter, applesauce, and erythritol until well combined.
3. Add in the eggs and beat until the mixture is smooth and creamy.
4. In a separate mixing bowl, whisk together the almond flour, cocoa powder, baking powder, and salt.
5. Gradually add the dry ingredients to the wet ingredients, alternating with the almond milk, and beat until the batter is smooth and well combined.
6. Spoon the batter into the prepared muffin tin, filling each liner about halfway.
7. Place a few sugar-free dark chocolate chips in the center of each cupcake.
8. Spoon more batter on top of the chocolate chips, filling each liner about 3/4 full.
9. Bake for 15-20 minutes or until the cupcakes are set and a toothpick inserted into the center comes out clean.
10. Remove the cupcakes from the oven and let them cool for a few minutes before serving.
11. Optional: You can also sprinkle some chopped peanuts on top of the cupcakes before serving for added crunch and flavor.

Diabetic Apple Spice Cake

Ingredients:
2 cups almond flour
1/2 cup coconut flour
2 tsp baking powder
1 tsp ground cinnamon
1/2 tsp ground nutmeg
1/4 tsp ground ginger
1/4 tsp salt
3/4 cup unsweetened applesauce
1/2 cup unsweetened almond milk
1/4 cup coconut oil, melted
3 large eggs
1 tsp vanilla extract
1/2 cup erythritol (or other low-calorie sweetener)
1/2 cup diced apples
1/4 cup chopped pecans (optional)

Directions:
1. Preheat the oven to 350 degrees F (175°C) and grease a 9-inch cake pan with cooking spray.
2. In a large mixing bowl, whisk together the almond flour, coconut flour, baking powder, cinnamon, nutmeg, ginger, and salt.
3. In a separate mixing bowl, whisk together the applesauce, almond milk, melted coconut oil, eggs, vanilla extract, and erythritol.
4. Gradually add the dry ingredients to the wet ingredients, whisking until the batter is smooth and well combined.
5. Fold in the diced apples and chopped pecans (if using).
6. Pour the batter into the prepared cake pan and bake for 30-35 minutes or until a toothpick inserted into the center of the cake comes out clean.
7. Let the cake cool completely before slicing and serving.

Lemon Yogurt Cake

Ingredients:
1 1/2 cups almond flour
1/2 cup coconut flour
2 tsp baking powder
1/2 tsp baking soda
1/4 tsp salt
3/4 cup plain Greek yogurt
1/2 cup unsweetened almond milk
1/4 cup coconut oil, melted
3 large eggs
1 tsp vanilla extract
1/2 cup erythritol (or other low-calorie sweetener)
1/4 cup fresh lemon juice
1 tbsp lemon zest

Directions:
1. Preheat the oven to 350 degrees F (175°C) and grease a 9-inch cake pan with cooking spray.
2. In a large mixing bowl, whisk together the almond flour, coconut flour, baking powder, baking soda, and salt.
3. In a separate mixing bowl, whisk together the Greek yogurt, almond milk, melted coconut oil, eggs, vanilla extract, and erythritol.
4. Gradually add the dry ingredients to the wet ingredients, whisking until the batter is smooth and well combined.
5. Fold in the lemon juice and lemon zest.
6. Pour the batter into the prepared cake pan and bake for 30-35 minutes or until a toothpick inserted into the center of the cake comes out clean.
7. Let the cake cool completely before slicing and serving.
8. Optional: You can also make a simple glaze by mixing together 1/4 cup powdered erythritol and 1-2 tbsp of fresh lemon juice until smooth. Drizzle the glaze over the cooled cake before serving.

Diabetic Vanilla Orange Cake

Ingredients:

1 1/2 cups almond flour
1/2 cup coconut flour
2 tsp baking powder
1/4 tsp salt
3/4 cup unsweetened almond milk
1/4 cup coconut oil, melted
3 large eggs
1 tsp vanilla extract
1/2 cup erythritol (or other low-calorie sweetener)
1/4 cup fresh orange juice
1 tbsp orange zest

Directions:

1. Preheat the oven to 350 degrees F (175°C) and grease a 9-inch cake pan with cooking spray.
2. In a large mixing bowl, whisk together the almond flour, coconut flour, baking powder, and salt.
3. In a separate mixing bowl, whisk together the almond milk, melted coconut oil, eggs, vanilla extract, and erythritol.
4. Gradually add the dry ingredients to the wet ingredients, whisking until the batter is smooth and well combined.
5. Fold in the orange juice and orange zest.
6. Pour the batter into the prepared cake pan and bake for 30-35 minutes or until a toothpick inserted into the center of the cake comes out clean.
7. Let the cake cool completely before slicing and serving.

Diabetic Chocolate Mint Cake

Ingredients:
1 1/2 cups almond flour
1/2 cup unsweetened cocoa powder
2 tsp baking powder
1/4 tsp salt
3/4 cup unsweetened almond milk
1/4 cup coconut oil, melted
3 large eggs
1 tsp vanilla extract
1/2 cup erythritol (or other low-calorie sweetener)
1 tsp peppermint extract
1/4 cup dark chocolate chips

Directions:
1. Preheat the oven to 350 degrees F (175°C) and grease a 9-inch cake pan with cooking spray.
2. In a large mixing bowl, whisk together the almond flour, cocoa powder, baking powder, and salt.
3. In a separate mixing bowl, whisk together the almond milk, melted coconut oil, eggs, vanilla extract, and erythritol.
4. Gradually add the dry ingredients to the wet ingredients, whisking until the batter is smooth and well combined.
5. Fold in the peppermint extract and dark chocolate chips.
6. Pour the batter into the prepared cake pan and bake for 30-35 minutes or until a toothpick inserted into the center of the cake comes out clean.
7. Let the cake cool completely before slicing and serving.
8. Optional: You can also make a simple glaze by melting 1/4 cup of dark chocolate chips with 1-2 tsp of coconut oil in the microwave, stirring until smooth. Drizzle the glaze over the cooled cake before serving.

Diabetic Chocolate Hazelnut Cake

Ingredients:

1 1/2 cups almond flour
1/2 cup unsweetened cocoa powder
2 tsp baking powder
1/4 tsp salt
3/4 cup unsweetened almond milk
1/4 cup coconut oil, melted
3 large eggs
1 tsp vanilla extract
1/2 cup erythritol (or other low-calorie sweetener)
1/2 cup chopped hazelnuts
1/4 cup dark chocolate chips

Directions:

1. Preheat the oven to 350 degrees F (175°C) and grease a 9-inch cake pan with cooking spray.
2. In a large mixing bowl, whisk together the almond flour, cocoa powder, baking powder, and salt.
3. In a separate mixing bowl, whisk together the almond milk, melted coconut oil, eggs, vanilla extract, and erythritol.
4. Gradually add the dry ingredients to the wet ingredients, whisking until the batter is smooth and well combined.
5. Fold in the chopped hazelnuts and dark chocolate chips.
6. Pour the batter into the prepared cake pan and bake for 30-35 minutes or until a toothpick inserted into the center of the cake comes out clean.
7. Let the cake cool completely before slicing and serving.
8. Optional: You can also make a simple glaze by melting 1/4 cup of dark chocolate chips with 1-2 tsp of coconut oil in the microwave, stirring until smooth. Drizzle the glaze over the cooled cake before serving.

Diabetic Lemon Lavender Cake

Ingredients:
1 1/2 cups almond flour
2 tbsp coconut flour
2 tsp baking powder
1/4 tsp salt
1/2 cup unsweetened almond milk
1/4 cup coconut oil, melted
3 large eggs
1 tsp vanilla extract
1/2 cup erythritol (or other low-calorie sweetener)
2 tbsp dried culinary lavender
2 tbsp fresh lemon zest
Juice of 1 lemon

Directions:
1. Preheat the oven to 350 degrees F (175°C) and grease a 9-inch cake pan with cooking spray.
2. In a large mixing bowl, whisk together the almond flour, coconut flour, baking powder, and salt.
3. In a separate mixing bowl, whisk together the almond milk, melted coconut oil, eggs, vanilla extract, and erythritol.
4. Gradually add the dry ingredients to the wet ingredients, whisking until the batter is smooth and well combined.
5. Fold in the dried culinary lavender, fresh lemon zest, and lemon juice.
6. Pour the batter into the prepared cake pan and bake for 30-35 minutes or until a toothpick inserted into the center of the cake comes out clean.
7. Let the cake cool completely before slicing and serving.
8. Optional: You can also make a simple glaze by mixing 1/2 cup of powdered erythritol with 2-3 tbsp of fresh lemon juice until a thick glaze forms. Drizzle the glaze over the cooled cake before serving.

Diabetic Caramel Apple Cake

Ingredients:

1 1/2 cups almond flour
2 tbsp coconut flour
2 tsp baking powder
1/4 tsp salt
1/2 cup unsweetened almond milk
1/4 cup coconut oil, melted
3 large eggs
1 tsp vanilla extract
1/2 cup erythritol (or other low-calorie sweetener)
2 medium-sized apples, peeled and chopped
1 tsp cinnamon
1/4 cup sugar-free caramel sauce

Directions:

1. Preheat the oven to 350 degrees F (175°C) and grease a 9-inch cake pan with cooking spray.
2. In a large mixing bowl, whisk together the almond flour, coconut flour, baking powder, and salt.
3. In a separate mixing bowl, whisk together the almond milk, melted coconut oil, eggs, vanilla extract, and erythritol.
4. Gradually add the dry ingredients to the wet ingredients, whisking until the batter is smooth and well combined.
5. Fold in the chopped apples and cinnamon.
6. Pour half of the batter into the prepared cake pan, drizzle with half of the sugar-free caramel sauce, and then pour the remaining batter over the caramel.
7. Drizzle the top of the cake with the remaining sugar-free caramel sauce.
8. Bake for 35-40 minutes or until a toothpick inserted into the center of the cake comes out clean.
9. Let the cake cool completely before slicing and serving.

Chocolate Cherry Cola Poke Cake

Ingredients:
1 1/2 cups almond flour
2 tbsp coconut flour
2 tsp baking powder
1/4 tsp salt
1/2 cup unsweetened almond milk
1/4 cup coconut oil, melted
3 large eggs
1 tsp vanilla extract
1/2 cup erythritol (or other low-calorie sweetener)
1/4 cup unsweetened cocoa powder
1/4 cup cherry cola (sugar-free)
1/4 cup sugar-free cherry syrup
1/4 cup sugar-free chocolate syrup

Directions:
1. Preheat the oven to 350 degrees F (175°C) and grease a 9-inch cake pan with cooking spray.
2. In a large mixing bowl, whisk together the almond flour, coconut flour, baking powder, salt, and unsweetened cocoa powder.
3. In a separate mixing bowl, whisk together the almond milk, melted coconut oil, eggs, vanilla extract, erythritol, cherry cola, and cherry syrup.
4. Gradually add the dry ingredients to the wet ingredients, whisking until the batter is smooth and well combined.
5. Pour the batter into the prepared cake pan and bake for 30-35 minutes or until a toothpick inserted into the center of the cake comes out clean.
6. Remove the cake from the oven and let it cool for 10-15 minutes.
7. Using a fork or skewer, poke several holes all over the surface of the cake.
8. Drizzle the sugar-free chocolate syrup over the top of the cake, making sure it fills the holes.
9. Let the cake cool completely before slicing and serving.

Diabetic Toffee Chocolate Cake

Ingredients:

1 1/2 cups almond flour
2 tbsp coconut flour
2 tsp baking powder
1/4 tsp salt
1/2 cup unsweetened almond milk
1/4 cup coconut oil, melted
3 large eggs
1 tsp vanilla extract
1/2 cup erythritol (or other low-calorie sweetener)
1/4 cup unsweetened cocoa powder
1/4 cup sugar-free toffee syrup
1/4 cup sugar-free chocolate chips

Directions:

1. Preheat the oven to 350 degrees F (175°C) and grease a 9-inch cake pan with cooking spray.
2. In a large mixing bowl, whisk together the almond flour, coconut flour, baking powder, salt, and unsweetened cocoa powder.
3. In a separate mixing bowl, whisk together the almond milk, melted coconut oil, eggs, vanilla extract, and erythritol.
4. Gradually add the dry ingredients to the wet ingredients, whisking until the batter is smooth and well combined.
5. Fold in the sugar-free toffee syrup and chocolate chips.
6. Pour the batter into the prepared cake pan and bake for 30-35 minutes or until a toothpick inserted into the center of the cake comes out clean.
7. Let the cake cool completely before slicing and serving.

About the Author

Laura Sommers is **The Recipe Lady!**

She lives on a small farm in Baltimore County, Maryland and has a passion for food. She has taken cooking classes in Memphis, New Orleans and Washington DC. She has been a taste tester for a large spice company in Baltimore and written food reviews for several local papers. She loves writing cookbooks with the most delicious recipes to share her knowledge and love of cooking with the world.

Follow her on Pinterest:

http://pinterest.com/therecipelady1

Visit the Recipe Lady's blog for even more great recipes:

http://the-recipe-lady.blogspot.com/

Visit her Amazon Author Page to see her latest books:

amazon.com/author/laurasommers

Follow the Recipe Lady on Facebook:

https://www.facebook.com/therecipegirl

Follow her on Twitter:

https://twitter.com/TheRecipeLady1

Other Books by Laura Sommers

Egg Salad Recipes

The Chip Dip Cookbook

Zucchini Recipes

Salsa recipes

Traditional Vermont Recipes

Recipe Hacks for Dry Onion Soup Mix

Printed in Great Britain
by Amazon